Samantha Rigg

Inside
Happiness
Guided Lessons from Spirit
for Your Greatest Journey

Dear Pamela.

May the wisdom and energy
in this book flow through
you to bring love, joy &
happiness.

S Rigg.

INSIDE HAPPINESS: Guided Lessons from Spirit for Your Greatest Journey

Copyright © 2021 by Samantha Rigg

Editor: Jessica Bryan, www.oregoneditor.com

Cover Creation and Artwork: Gavin Benson

ISBN: 978-0-646-83138-1

This book is dedicated to
Jay C, Pat and John,
Keith, and Jay P.

"Go forth and seek the life
you came here to be.
Being is all there is, so maketh
now those things in your creation
from love, joy, and happiness."

SAMANTHA RIGG

Contents

Preface

Early in the morning, usually between one and four, I am awakened to connect with Spirit. Sometimes this involves writing. When I wake up, the words to be written are running through my mind, and I capture every one until Spirit tells me they are finished. The words spill out so quickly that I cannot pause for a break for fear of missing one, because each word is significant in its meaning and relationship to the lesson. At the time of writing, the words do not make sense to me, and when there are no more words left to write, I go back to sleep. When I awake later, I have no recollection of what has been written. I just recall the process of writing.

The words come to me without sound, and the need to write persists until everything has been recorded. I type the lesson diligently in the morning, ensuring that each lesson is written as it was given, word by word, unchanged. The lessons use old English and are often poetic in nature. Spirit also uses "he" and "his" frequently, which is an older, less "politically correct" way of referring to humans; this style has been retained because it is how the language came from Spirit. The lessons have been edited ever so slightly for clarity.

I believe the lessons are written in a way that only your Soul understands. If you open your heart when reading these lessons, you will feel a deep resonance within. These words are likely to be familiar, as if they were once known to you but were forgotten over time, while you were on your journey in human form. These words from Spirit will ignite an inner knowing that fuels the journey toward your Soul.

These lessons from Spirit are simple and straightforward. They set boundaries for living a simple, joyous life from the heart. There is an inner sense of peace that comes with living from the heart. It is the center of all that you are and all that you know.

The guidance from Spirit can help you connect with your Soul. I can promise you that if you follow the lessons given in *Inside Happiness*, your life will unfold in a way that you could never have imagined, (even though the changes may be subtle), because when you change within, the world around you changes too.

You are a creator. All creation is a form of energy, and energy creates from the formless. So, please guard your words, soften your thoughts toward your fellow man, and know you are more than human. You are part of all things and all things are connected to you. Be kind, be love, and be your most true self.

These lessons have helped me and many others live with love, joy, and happiness.

Samantha Rigg
Australia
15 December 2020

"From the moment we arrive, we fight the battle to be free, with the Soul to guide our journey."

SAMANTHA RIGG

PART 1:

Wake Up and
Begin Your Journey

Lessons and Guidance on How to
Awaken Your Inside Happiness
and Truly Live Life.

"Let there be light in your Soul that ignites the fire of living so you can be free."

SAMANTHA RIGG

Switch On Your Internal Guidance

The mind is complex and likes to create complexity of the simple. We create internal chaos when we give our power over to the mind. If the mind were all that was required to navigate life, we surely would not have been gifted with a Soul.

Our Soul is our sense of being, an inner guidance system that steers us through life much more smoothly than if we give our life path over to the mind. The Soul knows just what we need, and if we leave our self-governance to the Soul alone, our life will be a different journey.

Our training, by conformity, teaches us to work on the mind. But where can there be such a place that lets us work on our Soul? It certainly does not come to the forefront that we have access to such a place other than when we are in nature or advancing our virtues in the art of freeform creativity such as music, dance, and arts.

There are places within that we often never dare go – places where we store the past stories of our life and outside experiences that we seek not, but seem to, always draw upon when there are appropriate times.

These memories serve as your behavioral DNA, framing your judgment and behaviors. We should caution you because these memories of the past may be left to interpretations of the mind and limit the life you experience, or not experience.

Our parents' lessons are also carried forth because they are instilled as behaviors we ought to carry. Just as the family name lives on, so do the learned behaviors and experience. We trust that these behaviors will serve us well, but there is no telling what will come of it because the accumulation of what we do may have expired within the passage of time.

So…here we seek how life can feel so complex at this point, because from such an early stage in life we are given the cross of our name to bear. We carry our behaviors like hangovers from the past that govern and frame our experience.

How can this be, that something so obvious gets missed? Quite simply, because we switch off the internal navigation system we have been gifted, the one thing that is eternally ours. From the moment we arrive, we fight the battle to be free, with the Soul to guide our journey.

The survival rate of the Soul is few. If we were to place bets on opportunity to win over our minds, the odds to win would be low to nonexistent.

What must we do as humans to capture it back? To capture what is almost, dare I say, stolen. We must switch off, unplug, separate ourselves from all distraction that entertains the mind and let go of all the beliefs that form the junk of life, which we do not need, but hoard.

We need to let go of all that does not serve us, that which draws out the inner voice that seeks to keep us on the merry-go-round of monotonous living. Lest we not forget our birthright. Lest we not give it away. Lest we seek what we know and have eternally known from within, because within is our connection to purpose, to begin showing us the way forward without apprehension or concern. We shall step forward triumphantly when we let go of all that does not serve us, all that we were given as a rite of passage that came with our name.

* * *

Let it go and you shall have command over every moment in your life. You shall command freedom in your heart, as your heart beholds all the secrets of your being that have been forgotten with the passage of time.

Let there be light in your Soul that ignites the fire of living so you can be free.

"I am all that I am and all that I can be. Herein lies the truth of all things in creation."

SAMANTHA RIGG

Seek Sanctuary
from Within

There are things in the making that you create and that unfold before you so life can be an evolution of your Soul. You seek joy in the external but, alas, it can never last, because when you long for all things outside of yourself, you never fulfill the art of joy.

* * *

The art of joy comes naturally when we unplug from all that is external and seek sanctuary from within. Within is the place that is found in nature. Nature is the healer of all that we are, and it can stop the external desires with its profound beauty.

There are things that keep us from experiencing nature's gift of life, but we often give them precedence over the decision to be at one with nature. We see ourselves separate from the environment in which natural beauty fills us up, restores our energy, and reminds us that we are a part, one of the same of something greater, far greater than we know.

The drive to separate ourselves comes at a great cost, because we give all power to man's creations. These creations often seem advancing, but so far, they can never reach the things that have been formed with Mother Earth, as her creations began perfect in their making and evolve in time unchanged.

How can nature, which is ever-changing, remain the same and unchanged for centuries? It is simple in that what has been created since the beginning of time was so perfectly formed that the need to evolve only occurs with the unfolding of its external environment. Nature seeks not what is outside of itself, because it knows, as it has always known, its connection with all outside of itself. Nature knows its place in the creation of God.

This world in which we live takes pride in the journey of life and will see those things that push against its flow fall away.

* * *

Time is not of the essence here, but a virtue set by man to help him track his passage through his life, so he can feel he makes growth and achievement in his passage.

The passage of time keeps as a monitor of his decay and serves not well for anything other than a tool for control and governance of one man by another.

Let the passage of time only live for decay. Do not let time govern your life. Let your life be governed by the moments of joy you experience in simple pleasures, like those found in nature.

"Take caution about what you create, because creation is indifferent to the request."

SAMANTHA RIGG

Let Go of Pain

The sands of time maketh for lost memories. You cannot carry those things you store in your body's memory. It must be the evolution of all humans to seek to learn how to let go and release the pain inside so they can move forward with the life they are meant to live.

Opening your heart is always the right way forward. For you to be triumphant, your heart must be fearlessly open to receive the pain that is your pathway to healing the heart. Whilst this may not make sense in its entirety, that pain is experienced to heal.

The pain you carry needs to be felt, for the very reason that it can shine upon you a way out of the behavior that prevents you from living a full and honourable life in which to live your purpose as it unfolds.

Letting go of pain is what humans struggle to do, until you cannot contain yourselves. You explode, erupting in a tyrannical way that suggests to others you have no control over your lives. You are so blinded to who you are (your Soul) that you cannot contain the right way of doing things and you behave opposite to what others know.

To take the pain away, you express the situation to others. But alas, this takes you deeper into the well of solitude – deeper into the perceived problem you face.

"So…how do I escape the pain," you might ask? The answer is by becoming its opposite, allowing the pain to be felt and witnessed with compassion for yourself and then treading carefully until the pain shifts. It always shifts, but what you do with pain determines what unfolds next.

Many lessons in life are difficult to grasp in thy written words, but you can take comfort that these lessons can be felt in your heart. The knowing of what to do is just an unfolding. Sometimes you do not seek to be still in loving silence, even though silence is all that's required to heal. So…herein lies the source of your comfort to pain:

1. Give no thought of the cause of pain. Just recognize it for what it is – pain is a current of energy that rides through you, building up force until it eventually finds its way out or the momentum shifts to fade away.

2. Be alone and still. Be the observer of the emotion. Let that emotion sit outside of you and know it is just energy with no connection in any way, shape, or form to the being that is you.

3. Let there be one light within that you draw upon to release the pain by calling upon the light to heal all that you carry in the human body. Let this light be your solider, the gallant knight that comes to save your day. The knight with the Chalice to replenish your Soul.

The Soul is ever knowing of your journey and seeks you in your evolution, never giving you too much of a challenge you cannot bear. Your Soul lies dormant until you let it free to take you and carry you from all situations you cannot bear. It is just a matter of knowing who you truly are and calling upon yourself to shine through in moments of despair.

* * *

We never ask for guidance at the right moments, because asking is forgotten when we are building our storm clouds – the storm clouds that take us so deep we cannot seem to find our way back to our light, a place where we feel peaceful, safe, and calm; a place where all is rational and makes perfect sense.

We just need to remind ourselves that we are pure energy, and we create everything through energy, like it or not.

Take caution about what you create, because creation is indifferent to the request. Creation happily seeks to unfold our requests as gallantly as the knight that can save us. It can place us under attack, leaving us in a situation we cannot win because our opponent is as strong as we are. Our opponent is a reflection, the living version of a self-story that we carry. We cannot win this battle when we surrender to its cause: the darkness created in the storm of pain.

* * *

Take forward with you this lesson and seek to withdraw yourself at the very moment of knowing your pain is simply energy stored within. It has no power if you give it no purpose. It can pass if you place it nowhere and go into your light to be free.

"Love all things in equal proportion then you can know how to truly love."

SAMANTHA RIGG

Go Forward with Love

The celebration of life comes in every moment we allow ourselves to feel the joy within; the joy within ourselves so that we can be free – freer than a bird soaring in the sky. Our lives hold significant purpose in the evolution of mankind, and every one, every thing holds its place in the unfolding of life and life's purpose. No matter how long or what they do in this world, everything has its divine place and divine order.

As humans, we constantly seek for more and consume everything in our paths, but the circumference of our life reach is limited to what we know through our senses. We cannot and choose not to see beyond what can be heard, seen, and smelled, because fear of dogma keeps us trapped in our cocoon. This is where the story of life is created. But alas, this mirage never lets us see the truth of what we are, and our potential of possibility fails to evolve into the light. We seek to exist in the commonplace, in a world created by the mind with man-made fiction to entertain us.

* * *

You are more than you know, and we seek you to rise-up beyond the dogma of life, extend your wings and soar once again to the heights you can reach but never dare. You must begin by questioning your existence and purpose for being on this journey, no matter what is unfolding before you. Elevate your attention and consciousness beyond all that is possible, beyond what can possibly be experienced in this human realm.

You are beyond the making of man. You are beyond body and mind. You are given the gift of life to create external sadness amongst yourselves so you can be free to feel the power of love and the eternal beauty that lies within.

As strange as it seems, the opposite of who you are is experienced to bring you home. This is why you see darkness evolving from human fellows – darkness all around, as man unfolds before your very eyes to be love.

Love is ever triumphant and always seeking evolution within you. Love can only be experienced when you fall apart to leave your core, your being. There can be no other love than the love of the mother – the mother is Soul. And Soul is the beginning of creation that is ever eternal, seeking out life, seeking to unfold itself from the human body for creation into a separate form where it can be in harmony with all things, as this is what it naturally came here to do and be.

Beyond human form lies the consciousness you seek, and all shall find themselves returning to the formless.

The formless is created in your minds as we seek our evolution and unfolding.

Take care of thy heart whilst on your journey, as it is where the Soul resides. Cherish thy heart and seek to find gentle compassion for all things and in all your doings to man.

He shall not fail you if you approach life with compassion, and you will see your life unfold differently if you just try this now.

Herein lies this lesson:

Go forth with an open heart, not a heavy hand of judgment.

Go forth with the core of your being, meaning know who you really are beyond this human form and get in accordance with your heart. Let life unfold. Do not push against the grain, or the sands of time will escape you and your life of loss, pain, regret, and suffering will be the frame of your experiences. It never has to be this way for any of you.

Take joy in knowing you are an eternal being. Take joy in every moment and know that the pain and suffering you create is a way of freeing, a way of causing separation from the human body.

Take pride in knowing you are from a single source of all creation. You are one and the same being, beyond human comprehension, beyond what is possible to fathom or create here in written word, as your level of understanding cannot take you past this realm until you leave it. Then you will find your understanding of what has been left out of these written words, as our means of connection now is to show you the way forward in life and how to live with simplicity and abundance – an abundance of joy and happiness wherein you are free from the suffering you create and the love of your Soul can shine through.

There are opportunities to connect with who you really are at every moment, but the fear of knowing your truth prevents you from daring to reach for the dizzy heights of the Soul. Your evolution forces a new way of being in which reliance on thought to solve your problems is much less commonplace and your Soul will begin to shine through.

We are pleased in the creating of all things, as all things are known to us. We sit outside of man's reach, beyond what can be known to him. We speak in words he can comprehend here, so he can once again come to understand his language of universal love.

No more destruction of pain can be created when he knows his true source. His source of life will set him free so he can be once again the creator he came here to be.

"Seek not what exists outside of yourself as all is known from within."

SAMANTHA RIGG

Seek First from Within for Creation

The gift of life is given by free will. The will to live free of all human virtues, whilst your time here on this earth is unfolding, is a commitment of an entirely different nature. The nature of all things is to grow and evolve but some (whilst very few) are chosen here to take the Chalice and Throne, for it is the course that sees them through life as an eternal being.

Living for the morrow will not suffice any human, as the morrow seeks not to serve them well. It takes time for humans to grasp the concept of living in the present, as now is all there is, so a reprogramming is required for humans to evolve beyond their thinking of the morrow and embrace their present day.

Seek not things outside of yourself but seek first from within as this is the creation of all things – all things must first flow through you in order to be received. Therefore, it maketh common sense that if you lack, then such lack should surely come from within, as within is a reflection of who you are, and thus shown its true representation in the outer world.

You seek forth all that is known to you with the senses, and, thus, the creation is in limit and finite in its ability to please or evolve you.

Creation is on a grander scale. Thus, what could possibly be grander than the transformation of thy human self into the true form of being that you are? A Soul amongst the shadows of life no more, as you triumphantly set yourself free.

Seek not, dear humans, what is sought and seek not what you see with your senses alone, but throw caution to the winds of the morrow and become the creator from thy eternal heart – the gift you were given for your reason to be living.

Throw caution to the past, we say, as it will not serve you well. Even the momentary being of service will seek to cause you harm as it acts as a distraction from your true path. A distraction, dare I say, is all there is to throw you off your course, because the courses set are weak and feeble, subject to turmoil, taking you from your path with such ease that in such a moment you forget what you came here for, and thus fail to live out your purpose.

"So…how do I stay on path and live out my purpose," you may well ask? By this our answer is simple. Stay true to the inner compass that guides you as your loving Soul takes to steer your ship home at any allowable moment.

Take course on your life and learn to live from the takings of your Soul, as there is no greater purpose or reason for being here right now on this earth other than this very journey of which we speak.

Let nothing, no one, break your course. Let life unfold before you with unwavering thought. Stay in focus of your plight, as your commitment to the Soul is eternal and shall not be broken, as it is what you came here for, and as other great humans have done so before you. Once the commitment or course is set, there shall be no other journey of which you are capable.

The wanting for the life of the morrow shall cease as you take up your Chalice triumphantly. Taking up your Chalice is the final foundation to your Soul. It is the bridge between heaven and earth and the closest place to being your eternal creator.

Do not give up the day for the morrow, but seek to hold on to all that you know. Take it upon reflection and let it all go. By letting go, this human consortium of life becomes the frugal makings of man that cannot reach the dizzy heights of the Soul, but far greater reaches where your consciousness lies. Yes…here I take you further than the Soul as your mind now boggles with possibility. So few can comprehend this possibility. But alas, all thy words seek to give instruction to what you all already know but have chosen to forget. As this information is your given birthright, it is here for the taking if you just choose to listen within and take up the Chalice of your creating.

Do not stray too far from your Soul, the inner guidance system you were gifted, because your Soul will only take to battle for you when it knows the possibility to win is ahead, or seemingly the Soul lies dormant awaiting your return. It is known to you as your navigation, so learn to trust within to reach it. Switch it on. Switch on the Soul of life to experience a greater journey than you have ever known – a journey vastly different from the one you have created in your human form.

Just take up the Chalice of Life and move forward from monotony and the dogma of the human race.

We seek out your evolution whilst you are here. We seek it so we all can grow and prosper in life's unfolding pattern of love in the making – life's unfolding journey of love. Love and harmony of all things created, all things forgotten, and all things now made. Be Love.

> "Go beyond our senses is necessary to reach our desired goal for freedom."

SAMANTHA RIGG

Stay on Course

The miracles of life are often gifted at times when needed. They creep upon you as a surprise, but you created them all the same. Knowing what you want and allowing things to unfold is the making of all creation. Your given birthright to let life unfold in such a manner is pleasing to all.

Mother Nature seeks to let the earth grow and develop as its natural cause. She allows all things to hold their rightful place in the universe of love and joy.

Life can seem cruel to humans, but they cannot understand what is required of them as they seek guidance from outside of themselves, which is just interference in the grand scheme of their lives. This interference causes pain and discomfort along the way because they have set themselves off course – the course they often need not travel to get to the destination they are going to. This is when humans look back on their path and reflect upon the miracle of how they got there. There is simply a deviation from their course. As in Mother Nature, as in all things, the course is always set. One way or another, you will always get to where you need to be, with or without sacrifice and pain.

No more lackluster life, because you are the creator of worlds seeking out harmony within, and this (as with all things) is what sets you apart.

There can be only one path you choose, one path that will be waiting for you, one path to take you home. It can be journeyed early in life, when life is joyful, or found later and traveled only a short way, for the journey was riddled with pain and suffering, which need not pave the way.

Take up the Chalice of your Soul's journey. Seek not into the dogma of life and you shall see no more pain and suffering. You shall see your journey unfold before your very eyes with tiny miracles happening all around. Such miracles take you further into your life as it unfolds with love and joy.

Take heed to thy words, as your mind is sluggish to grasp the concepts here. Take heed and free yourself from the dogma of life.

"We chase what is externally ours: the gift of life we already have and have forgotten."

SAMANTHA RIGG

Lead from Your Soul

As the sun dances amongst the trees, the light of your life unfolds before your very eyes. If you dare not blink, you shall never miss a moment. However, if you sleep whilst you are awake, you shall never reach the dizzy heights of your Soul.

* * *

The life we choose to live, or not, is made from the constant evolution of our journey to the Soul. We take the short road and the long road in our attempts to reach what we already have in our very being. We chase what is externally ours: the gift of life we already have and have forgotten.

It is our birthright to live in abundance on this earth. It is our birthright to accept that we can evolve when we are at true peace within our very being. Our love for all things (not resentment) shines through when we live from our inner guidance system, our Soul. Our very being relies on us to take the Chalice and seek forward to what we only dare dream. The dream of knowing we are eternal beings, and the very art of creation sits at our fingertips, in every moment as we breathe.

* * *

Seek not for morrows, we tell you, as you cannot create from there. Seek only for the sense of being, in that you should know thy self from there. Your sense of being can set you free from all incessant wanting. It shall set you apart from your fellow man so you can create from the formless, where all creation takes place.

You seek to control life, but life is beyond your creating. Mother Nature sets your course. She governs your evolution as She seeks you to grow triumphantly. As you fight against the hands of time, you lose the creative forces – the very forces you seek to grow and evolve.

Stop now pushing and pulling your way through life. This makes for a fruitless, tiresome effort. It can never give you what you truly want and seek, because what you seek is known only to your Soul. So stop right now and start thy journey from within. Only then will your life unfold as it should, with the natural forces of Mother Nature propelling you forward to reach your eternal goal of creation. Letting go of the hands of time is your greatest challenge, as creation by the clock limits all creation, stifling your progress at every given moment.

The great humans who stood before you never raced against the passage of time, but always absolved in the process of creation to the formless and led the passage of time from their own making.

These humans created such marvels, some of which changed the course of life and the way of doing things for humanity. These creations are their God-given right, formed as part of their journey through life. They were given to those who dare let go of convention, those sitting outside of man-made conventions created by their fellows. The message here we seek to share is lead your life from your Soul, and you shall be free to create what you came here for – your birthright, your legacy, your gift that frees you from the dogma of the passage of time.

Be there only one light that governs your life, and let that light be all that you seek and follow. Let that light be the light of your Soul.

"You have love unknown to man as he cannot be the bearer of its creating."

SAMANTHA RIGG

Seek to Love
As You Are Loved

The sands of time maketh for all man's dreams, but as each grain slips through the hourglass, man seeketh to make things more rapid in reaching his material and status goal. Seeking approval from outside himself, he will never fulfill the journey of creation itself.

Let go of all that does not serve you, even people, you may ask. Let it all go and be not bothered by external things, because what you seek from the human Soul is enough. You are enough to maketh your journey alone. You are enough and connected to all that is and has ever been before you.

Life is unfolding at every moment, so wake up to your journey. Wake up to your plight and create the creations you came here for. Do not waste time with other people's follies. They are a mere distraction, a demonstration for and to your lack of self-commitment.

Seek out and grasp inspiration from nature's gifts, wherein simplicity takes you by the hands of time and all is forgotten in that very moment. You and the present are all there is.

Cease now what you currently seek and stop your incessant wantings. Seek only the truth of your journey in life. More so, seek to love as you are loved; seek to be joyful so those around you can lift off their burdens. And my final word is, seek your life's journey from your Soul at every moment. Your Soul is your guide for life.

Your Soul can be trusted to take you far toward your destination. Your Soul governs all that you seek to experience. It has planned out your dreams, those desires you were meant for, the realities of why you came to be.

Do not shy away from life's challenges when your Soul says it is okay to move forward. Be brave and be fearless in following the gentle and guiding commands of your Soul. It is your eternal guidance system, and it will do you no harm. Always trust in your Soul, because your Soul is all-knowing of who you really are and, thus, all-knowing in those things that are pleasing.

Make your way now to the light of your Soul and let it shine for you ever eternal.

"Freedom comes from releasing our story we tell ourselves."

SAMANTHA RIGG

PART 2:

The Unfolding of Life Is Cumbersome

Lessons and Guidance on How to
Awaken Your Inside Happiness
and Truly Live Life.

"Being the light of guidance in your life takes great courage."

SAMANTHA RIGG

Your Life Unfolding

The unfolding of life, as we have said, is cumbersome, because humans find their way often through the reflection of another's eyes – never stopping to think of their own convention.

Humans seek to shadow and mirror their fellow man in order to live with the vacuum and bubble created by society.

In times gone by, this has always been the case. The relentless search for outside approval is really all that is known, and when you seek and are given such approval, you once again feel the right to be whole. But such follies of the mind trick you into conformity, and you become wrapped in the dogma of life again – never able to grasp at your true purpose, never able to come to terms with the fact that all you need in this life is You. You are enough. Outside influences can never match the magic that lies within each and every one of you to guide you on your way.

Being the light of guidance in your life takes great courage to separate from all things in the order of creating yourself. Your true being is your gift to yourself so you can feel the joy of freedom that comes from your internal force of creativity.

Seek not the confirmation of others outside of yourself. Seek not their guidance or approval. Switch off the desire to be known by others and know thy self for approval. Let there be only one governing force that propels your life into action. Let that force be your Soul, and let it shine through to govern and guide you in creation.

You might ask at this point, "What happens to the importance I have placed on outside relationships?" Well…herein lies the answer, in that you will come to know yourself and all you are in a way that is beyond your level of current understanding. As you unfold, the time passes you by without your level of awareness. You let go of convention as you seek to be present with your thoughts.

Your thoughts turn to thoughts of creation that propel action forward. Your actions are a product of the Soul and thus fulfill your desires and thirst for life as you become the creator and giver of life – giving life to the internal force behind the human that propels you to exist.

Be all that you can be on this earth whilst in your human form, because what you seek is seeking you to unfold in man's eternal creation.

Be still, be silent, and seek within what you and you alone can only receive. It cannot be gifted to anyone else. Your purpose here is unique.

You are the only one who can fulfill your heart's desires. So, stop seeking outside of yourself and go within to find the creator.

* * *

If we take a new view of life and our role within it, we can see what we have come here for and the part to play that is uniquely our own, but yet we remain connected to all things.

Some of us grow and prosper in life and some of us hide away, but all contribute to the unfolding of man's journey, no matter what role they decide to play.

"Let not your wondrous mind go wild like the weeds in a forest."

SAMANTHA RIGG

Let Life Unfold
Without Force

The journey of life is one of challenges that seek us out at every moment for our growth. As we face each challenge, we unfold from the tides of our past to become the person we rightfully came here to be.

As all things unfold in our lives, the pressure for change and transformation bubbles within until we cannot contain ourselves and we are propelled to move forward, like it or not, in a direction we set from our mind.

* * *

Take caution to your needs and wants, which are bound by human desire, as they seek to last you a long span of time. You can create your futures from decades of repetitive thoughts that unconsciously spill around your mind. So, take here a word of caution about your ability to create. The powers within for manifesting your world are greater than you give credit.

There can be no wrong creation when you find your stillness within as your thoughts for the making are silenced. So…here you can see that point in time when you can begin anew in the process of creation.

Your life will unfold in a dignant way if you just let the course of its making flow through you, rather than pushing and pulling on your material desires.

Let all things unfold without the force of mind and you shall find an abundance of love and joy in all things you create.

Seek not for those things that tie you down. Seek not for those things that bring momentary fulfillment, as they are not (and never were) yours for the making.

Let your dreams be yours, and yours alone. Herein lies your place of happiness. From within is only known to you, so seek not outside of yourself for ideas on its creating.

You are the creator of your world. Your life experiences unfold before you as you allow, and as they should. But here is the point of which you need to be warned. If you take no charge of what you were gifted and idly float through life without using your forces of creation, then you shall be trapped in the dogma of life's creation – the life created by another. Therein lies the root and cause of great suffering and depression, as all your powers that lie within will be left to another's creation.

You are whole and complete just as you are and need not another to guide you. You seek comfort from another, but all you need is the comfort and connection from your Soul.

There is a place where deep within you know what is being said. You now seek to find your resolve and comfort in these words. But can they take you on the journey to your Soul when you know not what you are and your ability as a creator?

Study thy words, my fellow man, as all the answers to guide you to your Soul are here.

Let not your wondrous mind go wild like the weeds in a forest, freely reproducing at every moment the sun allows. Stop and be still here with me, and I shall show you the way if you just allow.

I am your eternal creator who sits alongside you at every moment. I see all that you are and are becoming, and I am joyous that you have decided to greet me here at this point, as now you are to know that your life is in your making and not in the hands of another.

"We challenge you to learn the art of stilling your mind in nature to reconnect with who you are."

SAMANTHA RIGG

Let Go to Become Life

The sun shines on you and you feel alive. You connect with another and feel alive. But when you let go of all you carry (your emotions from the past), you become life. Your pathway is clear and set out before you because you have cleared the way to move forward.

The challenges you face are often self-created from your ways of thinking and learned beliefs. If you step clear of your own doings, you can move forward within your own light.

We feel your light. It is your navigation system, your Soul. If you allow it to, it will govern what you experience, in addition to how your lives unfold. If you can learn to let go of all that does not serve you, then absolutely nothing can get in your way to bring you everything you seek, all you create.

Being on earth in a human form is a small part of an expansive journey. Some here may not grasp this concept of eternal life, just now, but as you evolve (and if it is your time) you will come to know that you exist for eternity.

Existence, as you know it, is where one life ends and another begins. It is a constant flow, a stream that is never-ending, propelled by Mother Nature to keep moving.

The force for growth is strong and demands all of your attention. She has no time for us to be still, because Her desire for you to evolve during your time on this earth is stronger than you can imagine. Her force for change creates an internal discomfort. It forces you to move forward with Her, or to resist and suffer your own internal pain – a pain you need not carry.

All we know is your life seems short and you are never quite sure of your eternal being, but there will come a time (even if not here) when you shall know the vastness of your true being.

Live not for the morrow. Take up the Chalice and Throne so you can live with a full heart, triumphantly whilst your time on earth exists.

Knowing yourself is somewhat part of your battle. Imagine, if you can, that all of a sudden you know your truth and nothing else. The truth would surely mean that all your concerns and worries would fall away like a distant memory.

We challenge you to learn the art of stilling your mind in nature to reconnect with who you are. We challenge you to take part in your life with a different voracity and stop living in lack without luster. Seek out joys in simple pleasure and appreciate all that you have and are given. For all that you have is rightfully yours and here for your life worth living.

Take forward thy words and note them well as you evolve (and will evolve) with all eternity before you. Do not feel that time is upon you and haste as this is not your virtue.

I say again: seek the stillness from your heart so you can be free once more. The stillness within is where all answers lie. You just have to remember how to play the game.

The game of life seeks your evolution, and the wheel will never stop turning. Seek out your Chalice and live by thy heart, as your journey is yours in the creating.

"Seek only what the morrow brings by way of your current creating."

SAMANTHA RIGG

Step Forward
to Your Evolution

Where all things begin, life unfolds at its making. We may not realize the path we are creating until it is journeyed.

We often seek what we have forgotten when each path comes to its end, and then we realize what we have forgotten about ourselves.

As eternal beings, it is vastly different to remind ourselves where we come from, but we insist on throwing ourselves into the ocean of life, and we often get washed away in the current taking us further from who we really are.

Seeking alignment with our creator helps us live in full, being our potential, not missing a moment to live our truth.

* * *

Seeking for the morrow never sets the path of love, but uncovers the current of anguish. In the tides of anguish, you may get surely lost, as the formless is subject to creating the needs and wants of others.

Seek not for the making of oneself. Seek only what the morrow brings by way of your current creating.

Remember that all you do and think about is the beginning of the end, and each creation ends as it is formed, making way for the very next.

Alas, you seek our guidance to know what you maketh is right. But, alas, there is no knowing of what you're creating, as each creation is formed one moment to the next.

We seek to caution that you guard your words and seek to share our thoughts in how here. Thy thoughts are clever and subject to influence. But when you are upon the silence within nature, then your thoughts are unencumbered. Being part of nature is where your creations are with the infinite possibilities that are bound to your being.

Living out your life is to merely exist, but taking life in your own hands, governed by your heart, is living a life worthy of man. So few step forward into the hands of the creator that they cannot see the life they are creating.

Distrust in God's making puts humans further back than just knowing that life is unfolding. If you bother to take the pedal off misery and let the light of joyous events pave your path, then you shall seek no more of the morrow as the present is worth thy living.

Stop here, stop now your unreasonable follies, and take heed of thy words. Make your path of attention to God's very creations that unfold in the natural world.

Be the governor of thy thought and seek not for the morrow. Be here, right now, in your very moment and every moment.

Lest not forget your divine birthright. Lest not forget your abilities in the making; the making of life as it unfolds is your artful gift in creating.

Seek not the morrow here, we say. Seek for the love of all mankind. As life unfolds, you will surely know what it is to be one with humankind. Lest us give praise to one another in all our glory, and lest us reach then the dizzy heights of thy Soul, through love is your way forward. Love's veil of confidence surrounds you, as you now become whole.

Whole and complete you are in your making. Whole and complete like no other in the creating. Believe in all your God-given gifts, and you shall seek not the morrow in its creating. You shall know the present – it is all there is. And past is but what? An illusion of the mind? Past is a folly of times gone by, and what a waste it is to dwell in it when you have such virtues in the present and evolving moment.

Be clear on thy words and take every living moment as if it is your last, as thy body is not ever eternal. Stop wasting your time here on this earth, even as your heart is calling for your creating.

Mother Nature seeks your expansion, so please move forward with ease and kindness toward all fellow man. Humankind seeks your evolution. Step forward into "Here I Am."

"Go forth,
not with a
heavy hand of
judgment, but
a heart that is
light and full
of love for all
things."

SAMANTHA RIGG

You Are the Creator
of Your World

In all creation there is more energy in motion than we can tell you here. You seek to know the secrets to life's journey but can only travel them well when you let go of all that you carry inside of you.

Seeking out the answers is a good way to start your journey, but taking the Chalice and Throne is all that is required for the past to be forgotten.

Seek not the morrow here, we say. Seek out your future from within the creation of time where future is a matter of your ability to construct your desires from action here in the now.

Seek your special friends on this journey through life. Seek them out, as none need to be traveled alone.

You can reach the dizzy heights of the Soul when your energy is full and switched on to creating.

Leave behind your old ways; let them be clearly forgotten as they seek to govern your present-day with memories that can be rotten.

You are near the pinnacle of life when you take part in its creation. As life flows further and faster this way, it is beyond what you could dream of making.

As your reality unfolds in a newfound and certain way, you stop seeking for the morrow and start to live in the joys of the day with creation removing all the human sorrow.

Creators are what you came here to be, so take it up, take up creation and see what "new" brings your tomorrow. You are (and only can be) the driver of this change from within. You are now ready with me to take up the journey of creation.

Give it just one chance, one opportunity to shift all things out the way so that you create your worlds with me, the creator of all that you have forgotten.

Thy words reign strong within your heart, as all who heed them here shall come to know. You are by far the master of your worlds, and creation right here and now decides your tomorrow.

Let's begin with clearing out the past by simply letting go – letting go of all that does not serve you so you can begin anew. A new beginning will set you free on a course that is yours in the making. Just stop right here to think of your dreams and let reality do the rest. Your life shall unfold in mysterious ways, so it seems that one's involvement in the creation is from such a place outside oneself. Just try right here, right now, as there is no time like the present for creating.

Okay…so we have given you carefully laid out plans, but it is surely your task for their making.

Go forth, not with a heavy hand of judgment, but a heart that is light and full of love for all things and humankind, full of joy for your fellow man and his worlds in the creating.

No more sadness shall you bring. No more turmoil as life unfolds now from your very heart. It is yours in the making.

"A love of all things beyond thy self; a deep love that only resides in your Soul."

SAMANTHA RIGG

PART 3:

Reach the Dizzy Heights Of Your Soul

Lessons and Guidance on How to Awaken Your Inside Happiness and Truly Live Life.

"Seek not what exists outside of yourself as what you know comes from within."

SAMANTHA RIGG

Creation

There are things in the making that unfold in life, but when life comes to a standstill, then what next? You think that the end of human form is the end of all things in our creating. But how could this surely be the case? Thy Lord is your devout Shepherd guiding you through life eternal. Like these words, or not, He resides in each and every one of us.

Seek not for the morrow as no sunshine shall it bring, only seek for the sorrow so you can allow your heart to sing. Sorrow whilst opposite of our true nature shows us a way to reach the elevated heights of the dizzy Soul, whilst we enjoy such a brief moment here on this earth planet.

Lest your heart soar and lead thy way through life as you cannot be forgotten, as all your creatings cannot be rotten. Seek here your troubles to know you well. Seek here your trouble for your mind to dwell.

Wallowing in bygone days you seek to know your morrow, but alas you drown deep in your sorrow. Seeking, wanting, and continually searching. Why, my dear human child, can you be not still enough to cease your incessant wanting?

Let your heart be still so you can come to see your life as it unfolds is pure and clear like the oceans of Tibet. We seek to take you to further realms, but your mind is lazy and limits your path. Forget all that you have gotten, forget it now, as it is surely rotten.

Tibetan Monks carry all that you seek. They are the seekers that sought all that you need. They know the lessons of life here on earth. Take heed to their practices as they seek you well.

No push, no pull at yonder.

No give nor take.

No loss to spare as it is all here seeking your evolution.

Evolution of man is cumbersome. Evolution of Human is Dante in the making of follies. You gain to seek out yourselves, but your seeking is lost and always fails, as seeking is a plight by the mind that takes you far from your journey.

"Be your Heart," you hear us say. Be your heart and you shall know no morrow. Let thy heart soften the blows of life; let thy Soul live for every moment, let thy Soul shine in all its glory as the day unfolds. Let your heart be thy Chalice to heaven, as God does not wait for you there, as God lives here within you. He is with you at every given moment. He never leaves your side. He is ever-present, ominous in his glory. Set yourself aside to praise Him. He shall know you well. He shall take your Chalice, and He shall see you free of your cumbersome follies.

Guard your time whilst here on earth from the makings of other men. They seek not to understand your given gifts; they seek to know what creates other men. This fruitless obsession with knowing all things limits their capacity to know just one, and that one thing is God in your creating – it is subject here to none.

He is the almighty creator of all that you see, and He sees all that you are creating.

* * *

He who knows not what the morrow brings can surely seek his creating. There shall not be one moment, dear human, when we are not by your side, as thy heart ever eternal is in your creating. Let all things go now and go forth with your living to take upon one gift that is yours in the creating. And that is your gift of truth you can give to this world – the truth that you are here for the creating. Creating is the zest of life, the spoken word not given, the true faith it needs for its creating.

Do not follow, do not seek out to replicate, do not seek out from another your gifts. Go forth in your very own way and let your life be thy gift. Let your life unfold with thy Lord by your side. Let thy life be your way forward.

Hold tight your Chalice and be with God. Hold tight your Chalice here, my child. Have no fear; we love you. We have always loved you, human. Oh, human, we do not leave your side. Can you not see us all here with you now as you write? We love you now and for all eternity. There is no separation.

Be still enough to feel us here. We see you breathe; we hear your heart breathe; the warmth of life as it flows through you. You are a creation of our almighty God. He has not and will not forsake you.

"Sit here in peace with me for I am all you know and all that you need to know."

SAMANTHA RIGG

Connection

All is given when we just let life flow through us. It is a continual evolution of oneself that allows this to occur. When we seek what is known deep within, our Soul can guide us forward. The forward journey is traveled free from the pain and suffering created from our mind, as the mind is not in our way.

* * *

Keep thy words here close to your heart and look at all things in a different way. Do not let the dogma of life drag you down. Simply connect with your true self each day. If you make connection and focus, then you shall surely come to know the sense of being – the sense of joy that comes from deep within.

Take charge of thy mind. Do not let it stray. Do not let thy thoughts overgrow to consume your every moment, such that you cannot find the space where solitude and silence exist. Let your heart be your guide. Let your heart be full of joy, and you will find your way to the stillness that resides deep within.

Breathe deep now, my child. Do not let time slip away. Breathe deep until the breath is all of your focus. Take in every moment and know it is not your last, as last is forever for your Soul. Even here on earth you may know the joys of the Soul. It can be with you in every given moment if you dare to step inside of that place you have forgotten. Seek not your solitude from all beings but seek to connect with those in kind, and you shall know all it is to be human, once again.

The joys of life can be shared with another, but the sharing seeks to fulfill that void inside. Seek not to replace the loneliness within with such distraction, because the fulfillment will not contain to lasting joy.

When there is a connection with who you are, all other connections can be enduring, joyful, and triumphantly complete in their making.

"We learn to know our truth and begin to live when we go deeper than we imagined possible."

SAMANTHA RIGG

Evolution

You come to know in time the nature of all things, and with time a journey that once occupied your hearts and thoughts is once again forgotten, a distant memory, but alas it can regretfully reappear at any given moment with a trigger from an event but external.

The life you live is but an accumulation of events, of things that you collect on your journey. There can be no greater challenge in life to let go of those things you accumulate, as the hanging on seems to let you believe and think that things are as they always were. But alas, this is not and never can be the case for each and every one of you. Because – as with all creations in Mother Nature's grasp – she seeks your continual evolution, like it or not. She seeks your continual expansion and growth eternal.

So herein lies your lesson, in that you have to learn to let go of those things you carry and hang onto for the higher-order in your evolution will continue to push all things forward, as life (your life) is but a greater expansion of every given moment.

"How do I deal with the letting go," you may well ask? For herein lies the truth of human failings when one feels stuck, or so it seems. But alas it is the point of all your creating. It is what you do in those moments of desperate clinging to what was that creates the next of life's unfoldings. You now show gratitude for all you have and all that was, but surely the next great thing is there for the creating.

Do not get swamped and stuck in the evolution of life as you shorten your time in the creating. Do not give up on Mother Nature's gift of evolution, as it is yours in the creating.

All shall be shown to you as your path is clearly set – the course is given at your making. So, throw caution to the wind and embrace the change of evolution. Be part of what you are creating. Be the creator of your worlds. It is what you came here to be. Do not give it up to another; do not let that be.

It is here, right now, that you owe it to yourself to be part of the tapestry of life's creating.

"Do not give it up, do not give it up," you hear us say. Do not give it up to be part of its creating. The creating of your life is ever eternal, so do not miss a moment, not a single moment to be apart from its creating.

There cannot be but one thing you came here for as the Soul's evolution seeks through you an active form of creation. As a course set seeks to cause your energy in motion that equals all your creation, then we see life's unfolding pattern in its tapestry.

The tapestry is your story, but it need not be looked at in parts, as humans often do. The whole is but the journey and the parts are pieces of you. Those pieces of your learning that are the colors you show. The colors are your emotions that you just cannot and will not let go. So, when all is said and done and your tapestry is on show, how are the colors of your final piece, your life's creation going to show?

You are not a passenger in this life. You are the creator. You hold the needle and thread that creates every moment. You hold all the pieces that will be your final works in the life that is ever-evolving. Make sure what you have left on display, your tapestry, is full of colorful beauty as you are all that you see in nature. So, just make sure you are one of the same – the same you are, mankind, not separate from all given things. There is no separation between you and that ant you see. We are all part of One thing. Be not forgotten who is your maker, as your maker is seeking you – mark here thy words that your creator lives within each and every one. Even the ant you see on your path, you are all one of the same. And when your time is done here on this earth, you will come to know His claim. So, be good to fellow mankind and all the creatures of this earth, as we are all connected and benefit greatly from your time on this earth.

"There is always something you can do to change the order of things in your life."

SAMANTHA RIGG

Begin

In the beginning, where all creation is made, lives your Soul. In the middle or center is where all that you are exists. You are the center of all things that gravitate around you whilst your time here on this earth is short. You must make sure that you live with those things around you that help you survive.

Seeking and wanting too much is not of your true nature, as all that you need comes from the core of your being.

When you copy, ask, and seek answers to your life from outside forces, you lose the power of your own creation. To exist in another vacuum is all that can then exist for you.

Do not throw it away, this time on earth, by limiting your ability to create. Do not throw away your opportunity to know your vast potential.

Give it a try; just listen within to your Soul – that soft, inner voice is calling, awaiting your arrival at any given moment, if you would just step inside to listen.

"Here I am," we hear you say, and we are heeding to your calling, as we see not your doings, only those things left undone.

Take charge of your life now, my child, as it is yours for the creating. Do not dilly-dally to the finish line. Make it your race. Run triumphantly with steadfast speed to the length of every journey, as you will take up thy Chalice and Throne.

Take forward life's lessons and know life is externally evolving. Do not waste time on the morrow, as creating is but a virtue of any given moment.

Lest your life be the victory of your Soul, so you can live joyously from thy heart, as thy heart is the governor of your creation. It is the barometer of how well you live and experience life whilst here on this earth.

Be the candle that carries the light for others, showing them the way. Be your governing light like no other. Be the Soul that guides all on their way. Be here now with me as you shall know no harm. Be all that you can be. Be here with me still in ever-loving silence to know thy self once again.

There cannot be any other than your journey – this journey you take is yours alone. So, let go of what you carry and come to know thy self, as all that you seek is seeking you now.

Let go and create space for all you are creating, as creating seeks out its maker of creation.

Lest it be so that you come to know thy self well. Lest it be so that you are the seer of all creation in your external world. Lest it be so that you know your self once again and you can finally be free to know and live all that has been forgotten.

At this point, life becomes simple, with the ease and flow of creating basking all around you; dancing in every moment at your arrival, triumphantly following in your awakening, glistening, shining, beautiful creator. You seek no more when the seek reaches the seeketh. No morrow shall you seek; it is all within your external creating. Here now is where your life begins.

"Your evolution takes a vast amount of energy when you leave its workings to your mind."

SAMANTHA RIGG

Begot or Begotten

There are things not forgotten by all people. Their birthright is a given gift and it is celebrated each year. Their knowing of whence they came here on this earth is never forgotten, but all that they carry is with them until they request their freedom; until they take up their plight to be free, find their freedom, and know their truth once more.

It is not an easy course to take, and one can knowingly stay blind from their truth. But truth always seeks the arising to the surface when it least not matters to all but the creator, the originator of lies that we tell ourselves. Let all those who challenge thy quest to reach the Soul know that it is a cause you shall not make lightly. Your path, riddled with turmoil, need not be carried.

You cannot be the carrier of all this burden of life pain, which your mind is joyously creating as it seeks to stop you from reaching that eternal journey.

The learnings and teachings of the mind are only useful by the great philosophers who seek to know things in their practical use. But for the average fellow, the mind can cast a bludgeoning blow for the way he lives and experiences life. "Begot or begotten," you hear us say, as your course is in the making – the making of all things past and all things in the creating of the mind.

"There cannot be any other journey than the journey to your Soul."

SAMANTHA RIGG

Reconnection

There are things you need to know that you seek to know and that is, all life is ever evolving. Like it or not, life seeks to evolve in a certain way.

You get stuck in the push and pull of life when you resist its calling, not making the necessary step forward to be part in its creating.

No more follies of the mind shall you create when you give up incessant wantings. And then, when there are no more wantings, what next? Life unfolds in a certain way for the benefit of all mankind. When the wind blows, the tree does move with it, not against, or it will surely break off its branches that it needs to live. So, human, do not sit idly in your woes – go with the flow just like the tree.

Take your time when you are unsure and seek not the direction of others in that day. But look for confirmation within, through stillness.

Seek to be still at all and many occasions, as stillness is where you will find no follies. Here in stillness you will come to see the point in your creation of how human form began.

Softly, silently, and peacefully does your Soul call your return. A longing at the separation you feel is the cause of your sadness. A reconnection with your Soul is your awakening to life (your eternal life), the force behind the wind that does blow thy tree.

Take up the follies of mind and let them flow through you without any volition. Let them pass and avoid becoming thy toxic thoughts. The poison and pollution of idle and untrained mind is not good for you or the evolution of mankind, as it seeks only destruction in its path.

Mind is but triumphant when working in full unison with thy Soul. Mind is but glorious when working out the doings of a day. But alas, mind cannot, will not and never will, be the life navigation system of thy Soul.

Let it be your Soul that decides what your life is for the making. And set all else aside for your mind, as the mind, of its own accord, is a specialist at creating the pathway that is instructional for the body into how to reach thy Soul's desire.

"Know thy self is the source of all freedom."

SAMANTHA RIGG

Power

Of all the things that you come to know in this life, one thing is certain: you cannot give in to the follies of others or you give your power away. You cannot throw your life away for the distraction caused by/from another's emotions.

We seem to be sponges for the energy of another, but what is it that we are absorbing? Is the other really feeling what we feel, or have they just cast off on a journey and left us behind with those things we cannot carry? Our feelings are subject to another's when we leave ourselves open. Our feelings are always going to be under such influence, and we will be left stranded when we come across such situations.

"So…how do we guard ourselves here," do you say? Stop to think that when another who crosses your path seeks to engage you in their journey. Are they seeking to drop off the things they no longer want to carry?

Dropping off old emotions left for you to collect so you can pick up the pieces they leave behind – so they can set forth on their journey and you can hold onto what they have let go. This transfer of ownership of energy is a fait accompli for those who wander around endlessly absorbing the matters of another's life.

It is not that you need an internal force field to hide behind, but just know that you are not here to be that sponge – that sponge, that caretaker of another's troubles, their energy that is oh so wrong.

Blow it off, cast it away with them, as it is not (and never was) yours to carry, and you shall see how little these people have control over your actions.

You will be untouchable by another when you just seek to stop such absorption of their energy. At that point, you become a useful part of their healing recovery. As you take up the force field, breaking the transfer, they have no choice but to let it go or carry it forward on their journey.

It sounds so simple. But how, may you ask, do you not get caught up in another's follies of the mind? Well… pay attention and know, my friend, that such follies are their journey to take and not yours to carry. Their journey is always for their learning and traveled alone. But by the very strength you have they shall but learn that their follies are of no use to anyone and discard them, leaving them behind. And then at that point, the transfer is not possible, as the forces of nature driving it forward no longer exist and you both can move forward triumphantly.

Seek to find solace and pride in your care for another, but decide not to be a sponge for the causes they carry. Let yourself be open but guarded to the forces of nature that come from within each and every one of us.

Be still, be silent, and question your role. Seek to understand that the only caretaker you can be is the one of your very own.

You cannot and will not control another, no matter how hard you seek to try, because one way or another your involvement will only cause you to challenge the situation, fueling it further. Soften their blow by giving it no power and allow them to see their very own follies. Stop, be still, and be silent. Amen.

For all can be solved from that very place. Take our words with you everywhere unless you do not care. For these words will help you all and cease the transfer of energy that is not yours in the making, so that others can learn faster on their journey of life's creating. Give up the follies of another by softening it with your love. Conquer all that another throws your way with an invisible force field of love.

"Go beyond
your senses
is necessary
to reach your
desired goal of
freedom."

SAMANTHA RIGG

Here I Am

There is a place within that you dare not go that seeks you at every moment. It is deep within and sits with all the shadows of life. Stay here with me now as we take you there, simply seeking out the sorrow that hides deep within so you can let it go to be free, so memories of the past do not hang around like decoration in your present day.

Letting go is of your own making. It cannot be done or enabled by another. This is but solitary work that you must seek to undertake yourself, without any interference of another.

Knowing your triggers in life can help you move past the emotions you carry. But triggers often are hard to handle, as they are already in the making. "So…what must I do," we hear you say, "…to reach inside to the places I dare not go? The places where I keep the emotions locked away that limit my present day?"

You must be brave enough to know that when you seek for truth from your own self-created emotions, you will then be able to pass through them with greater ease.

What do I carry that makes me feel this way is a good point of self-inquiry? Is this who I really am, or is it a wave from the current of my life that no longer serves me but still exists, causing ripples in my present day?

What would it mean if you had nothing of the past and only live with your present day? What would your life be like right now with just you and nothing in your way?

Yes, here is the point of contemplation that you should seek from your very self. Ask, "Who am I, but not just a Soul that seeks my own evolution?" Evolution is one part of a greater whole – part of all things coming together seeking expansion for your life external; seeking your growth for a new tomorrow; seeking your development to once again know the fullness of who you really are and what you came here to be.

Do not just give up on your quest to the Chalice and Throne. Make it your plight, your mission in life to seek out and clear out the internal junk of life past that you need not carry. Do not let it get in your way, as on the other side of everything there is the beauty that lies within. It is your gift that you came here to share. The delivery of your unique gift in this world is the becoming and being who you are and doing what you came here to be. Be love, my child. Life is in your making.

"Seek first to fill your heart and all other things you seek will follow."

SAMANTHA RIGG

Allow

The wonderment of life is ever abundant when you just let go and allow life to flow through you, rather than the push and pull of all things you fight against to be free.

- Guard thy words.

- Be kind.

- Do not fall into the dogma of life circumstances.

- Take time to get out into nature.

- Let your Soul decide your life – as you call it "follow your heart."

- Be free to choose what you think or do not think.

You are enough and need no other to define you, as your inner beauty will shine through once again as you come to know the formless in all things. When you are here at this point, the truth of who you really are cannot be forgotten.

Take up the journey to the Chalice and Throne, as all that you seek is seeking you – if you are willing to let go of all you carry inside, all you hold onto that no longer serves you. Just let go and come to know, by creating space within, who you really are and what you came on this earth to be.

You are divine, a divine creation of God. And as you sit right here, right now, you are in perfect creation just as you are.

We have such love and deep appreciation for you, my dear human. Go forth and live the life you came here to be.

"When we push against creation, we restrain our progress."

SAMANTHA RIGG

Energy in Motion = Creation

All in creation is the place where you begin – your lives are but an eternal journey spanning further than your human form. We are the formless here to teach you how to be human – be the human form creating in the formless. You were created through energy and all that you are is energy.

There are things here we tell you that are obvious to so few, until such a time that it is given consideration.

Think about the act of human creation – the energy in motion of human connection. When you begin the creation of human form, it is formless, and all that you come to be in a short space of time is form. Your creation of divine order is the beginning of your time on earth.

Your perspective here can change the course of your life if you dig deep to look inside and inquire as to who you really are. Can it be so obvious that it gets overlooked? Now here we stand by your side watching the glory of your learning and growth. Ever-expanding and evolving into the formless, here you create right now. Be thy watcher of your thoughts and take notice of feelings inside, as they in unison work to prevent you from knowing who you are.

"Why does it have to be this way," we hear you ask? Because the evolution of humans is cumbersome until you take charge of your mind. Then your life will begin to unfold in a certain way. When you learn that your inner self, your Soul, shows you the way, you will learn to listen within and not get distracted by the push and pull of life. At this point, you will reach the gateway. Your heart is the key to unlock all that blocks your way – to walk through the passage of heaven whilst here such a short time on this earth.

You can live as one within and as one you shall see your true connection to all.

All that stands in your way is you, and this is how it was always meant to be. Self-mastery through practicing the ways of life will lift the veil of uncertainty as to who you are. And then you set forth on your journey in a very certain way.

So…behold all of your given gifts and share them with the world. This is your reason for being. Just step forward into what you came here to be.

PART 4:

The Final Word, For Now

Lessons and Guidance on How to
Awaken Your Inside Happiness
and Truly Live Life.

Shifting Through the Fog

There are often times in life when everything seems to fall apart. This is the point when, if we are still, we can find the place of change. The direction from within is soft and subtle but often relentless in its approach to attracting our attention.

The past often gets in our way of moving forward as we seek out the memories that most often do not serve us well in our present day. At this point we fail to see how things can possibly go wrong in our present. We seek all those things that cause us pain and fail to place our full attention on the joys of our present day. We fail – to bring forward what we need not concern ourselves with – bring it into the light of day so it can be seen and felt by all that resides in our vicinity.

Sadness at this time is but a part of who we are. The frustration with life, people, and circumstance is often not discussed, although it sits at the surface for everyone to see, like it or not.

The fact that we cannot, will not, face ourselves and would rather freely handover our life path to another is of grave concern to many. Why it is that when your life is so important it can be gifted to another to decide so freely (what you cannot see) where you are going (with their guidance).

Let not those things that unfold in your life take charge in your present day. Let those things soften your life; let them slip between your fingers and do not follow anyone else, other than the beat of your own drum.

There is always something we can do to change the order of things in our lives. But what can be done here and now? What can be done to enable you to shift through the fog that surrounds your present day? Let go by putting your thoughts onto productive matters that seek to move you forward and thus away from the present circumstances you have outgrown.

Be joyous, knowing you can change your course with the single act of thought, as thy thoughts are but the start of creation on your journey.

Your evolution takes a vast amount of energy when you leave its workings to your mind. Its pull against all things makes for a longer journey than required.

Why is it, Human, that you do not heed our words when in the moments of turmoil your retched wild mind creates. Let it go now and let it be forgotten. Let it go. Your mind is rotten.

By Your Side, Always

Our love for you is but a virtue of time. Each second that lapses brings you closer to us. We watch and wait for your coming. In every moment we seek out your arrival. Oh, my Lord, he does wait by your side, knowing all that you seek and all that you are. He lets you wait as long as you wish, for His arrival seeks out your awakening.

Let yourself come to know your fears, and know that these fears are but a figment in time where your true self, your Soul, has been buried away.

You shall not go alone at any point on this journey through your life, as you shall know that all of what you seek is there awaiting your arrival.

What do you long for that creates so much sadness in your heart? Where your heart is all but complete, it should not be mistaken to feel this way, as your sorrow governs your present day.

Make way for us on your journey, as you know when we are here. Make way for this very reunion you seek but do not dare make clear. The way forward – in which we seek your growth, your evolution from human to the uniqueness of oneself – has existed for all eternity. Seeking your evolution and the truth of what you are is your place in God.

Be You
to Create Your World

In a world of infinite possibility, you create change from being who you are.

***

There comes a time when the realization of what to do and why becomes apparent, and at such a time you seek out with greater respect and virtue for the lessons given here in this book.

But our teachings are not mere follies for controlling your mind; they are but a virtue of how to manifest your life moving forward.

Let it be known to you that you can live happily from your own volition, again you hear us say, when you just step inside to listen. The voice – that inner dialogue – reigns loud and clear so you know exactly what to do to make life unfold in the way it should, taking the art of guiding your life from your Soul to a new dimension, to a new way of being.

Living up to your expectations then becomes simple and takes you in a new direction, a direction that has not been seen before by man, himself. The discovery and self-inquiry that begins will open up a new way of being, whilst you live out your life here on earth.

Take heed of thy words here, my child, as your heart often gets intertwined with the makings of another. Be still in silent solitude to carry out your life's work, your God-given gift, and be the creator of your worlds – the creator that you came here to be.

Wisdom with Life Unfolding

There are many virtues in life's unfolding that come with the passage of time. The decay of life brings us to a point at which we see clearly our way forward.

We seek to then stop grasping at indecent follies and start living with a firm grasp on how to live from the heart. Some here fail their plight and get lost in the sea of dogma, but there is always a chance, a single opportunity available to all seeking their rightful freedom.

Be brave and fearless, whilst your time here on earth is limited. Be the rightful Soul, the leader of your world and beacon of hope for others, for eternity awaits you. It is only around the corner, and at any given moment you may step inside Her grasp.

Be kind and be cheerful. Make time for Joy, as these things are free and give you the greatest pleasure.

***

If you would leave all things to us, they would surely be there for the creating. Creating is not of wanting things but putting into action the force of energy behind your gift and getting forward motion of the action to create new opportunities to reach your final goal.

About the Author

Samantha Rigg has been blessed with an inner dialogue from Spirit. This dialogue is kind, gentle, and always loving. Sam puts everything Spirit instructs into practice, which has helped her learn the lesson of allowing and surrendering.

She was connected to something that led to a wonderful and amazing, although unbelievable, new aspect of her life. The best part of the connection is that Sam, through working with Spirit, has become a conduit for positive changes in others through her gift of light. In her own words, she describes her connection with Spirit:

"It feels like everything is love, all is heart, and all is light. You are never alone. Spirit is sometimes funny and always encouraging and positively reassuring in a gentle and loving way. I am able to draw on the guidance of Spirit and happily live no matter what goes on around me."

For more information about Samantha, please see: www.samantharigg.com.au.

Printed in Australia
AUHW020909040121
339157AU00011B/46

9 780646 831381